EXPLORATION THROUGH THE AGES
THE TRAVELS OF LIVINGSTONE

Richard Humble

Illustrated by
Richard Hook

Franklin Watts
London · New York · Toronto · Sydney

© 1991 Franklin Watts

First published in Great Britain
in 1991 by
Franklin Watts
96 Leonard Street
London
EC2A 4RH

First published in the United States by
Franklin Watts Inc
387 Park Avenue South
New York, NY 10016

First published in Australia by
Franklin Watts Australia
14 Mars Road
Lane Cove
NSW 2066

UK ISBN: 0 7496 0366 6

A CIP catalogue record for this book
is available from the British Library.

Designer: Ben White

Series editor: Deborah Fox

Editor: Roslin Mair

Picture researcher: Sarah Ridley

Illustrations: Richard Hook,
Hayward Art Group

Consultants: John Robottom and our thanks to Bill
Cunningham at The David Livingstone Centre,
Blantyre, Glasgow.

Photographs: The David Livingstone Centre,
Blantyre 5, 6, 12, 22, 23, 26, 29; Mary Evans Picture
Library 25, The Royal Geographical Society 4, 28;
Zefa 19.

Printed in Belgium

**Words in bold appear in the
glossary.**

Contents

The "Dark Continent"   4
The making of a missionary   6
Learning from the Africans   8
A narrow escape   10
Across the Kalahari   12
The mighty Zambezi   14
West to the Atlantic   16
"The smoke that thunders"   18
The great lakes of Africa   20

Challenging the slave traders   22
"Dr Livingstone, I presume"   24
The last march   26
The "Great White Doctor"
dies   28
Glossary   30
Timechart   31
Index   32

The "Dark Continent"

Today it is hard to believe that only 150 years ago, most of Africa was hardly known to the outside world. Knowledge of Central Africa was no greater than it had been in the time of the ancient Greeks and Romans. To Europeans Africa was still the "Dark Continent", and little had been explored, with the exception of its vast coastline.

By the early 1840s, Europeans had penetrated only a narrow fringe of territory extending inland from the coast. Because they were very difficult for ships to use, none of the great rivers – the Nile, the Niger, the Congo or the Zambezi – offered an easy highway into the unknown heart of the continent.

In ancient times, Africa was thought to be the Earth's great southern continent, with the mighty River Nile as its central feature. How far south Africa reached, and exactly where the Nile had its source, were questions which fascinated geographers and explorers for many centuries. In the first century BC, Caesar, the Roman emperor, is said to have sailed far up the Nile, together with Queen Cleopatra of Egypt. But after Caesar's death it took another 1,532 years before the Portuguese sailor Bartholomew Diaz reached Africa's southern tip in 1488. And, nearly 400 years later, David Livingstone was still searching for the source of the Nile when he died in Central Africa in 1873.

In the 1840s, when Livingstone set sail, northern Africa and the east coast from Mombasa south to Sofala were controlled by the Arabs. In the south-west and south-east lay the Portuguese coastal colonies of Angola and Mozambique. Dutch colonists had settled Cape Colony in south Africa from 1652 to 1806, when it was taken by the British. By 1840 its restless population of Dutch pioneer farmers (**Boers**) had begun to move northwards, seeking lands free from British control.

Africa's greatest curse in the 1840s was still the trade in human slaves. Slaves were shipped from the west coast to the European colonies in the West Indies and America. European slave-traders made fortunes in this trade for some 300 years,

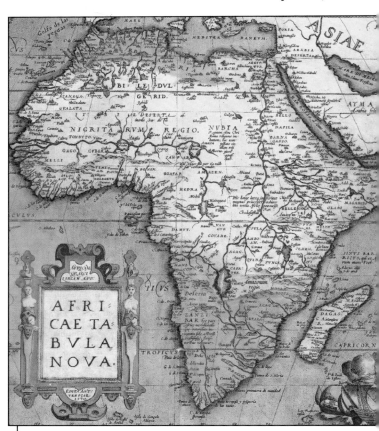

△ Here are depicted wholly imaginary lakes, rivers and mountains. This map of Africa was drawn in the the 1570s.

△ This drawing of David Livingstone is based on a painting commissioned by the London Missionary Society.

but eventually it was recognised as a great evil. It was abolished in all British colonies in 1834, but sailors from other nations continued the trade as there were still people willing to exploit the African people in order to get wealthy.

Africans were still suffering this cruel slave trade and the harshness of the Boers when a new wave of European invaders set sail, hoping to help rather than to enslave. These were the missionaries, teachers and doctors whom the young David Livingstone joined in 1841.

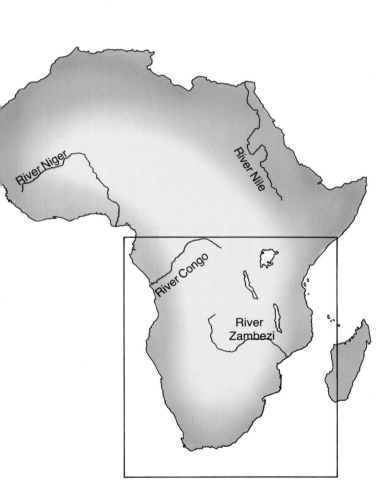

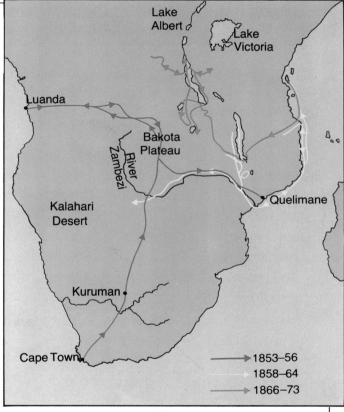

△ Southern Africa, showing the early missionary travels of David Livingstone.

◁ In the 1840s, this was almost all that the outside world had learned about the true geography of Africa.

The making of a missionary

Imagine growing up in a family of two parents and five children, all living, cooking, eating, washing and sleeping in a single room measuring no more than about 4 by 3 metres. This was the sort of house provided for the workers at Blantyre Mills, a cotton-spinning factory near Glasgow in Scotland in the early 1800s. It was in a room like this that David Livingstone was born on 19 March 1813, and it was his home for the first 23 years of his life.

Not that young David spent much time in the family room. Three-quarters of the workers at Blantyre Mills were children and, like them, David worked six days a week, from 6 o'clock in the morning to 8 at night amid the steaming heat and roaring machinery of the mill. Crawling and climbing between the machines, his job was to keep the cotton spindles fed with smooth, unbroken thread. Sometimes he covered up to 32 kilometres in a day's work. Few of the children had the strength to study at the classes held in the company school, but David Livingstone was one of the few. From 8 o'clock to 10 each night he spent every possible minute reading, and his greed for study astonished his teacher. At the age of 13, he was the only pupil at an extra Latin class held by the village schoolmaster.

Under the eye of his father, Neil, David Livingstone grew up in a strict God-fearing family. From religious writings he learned of the growing need for missionaries to preach Christianity in faraway lands. His endless reading also taught him about the latest discoveries in science and medicine. By the time he was

△ The actual room the Livingstone family lived in at Blantyre near Glasgow.

▷ At the headquarters of the London Missionary Society, the young Livingstone is shown his destination in South Africa – Kuruman. The mission station was founded in 1821, but had made very few converts.

21 years old, David had decided that his life's work should be as a medical missionary. It took 18 months of hard work in the mills to save the money needed to pay for his studies to become a doctor. For a nineteenth-century factory boy, it was an amazing achievement.

David's medical and missionary training lasted from 1836 to 1840. These were lonely years in which only his strong will carried him through. But at last the years of study ended, and he was accepted by the London Missionary Society. In December 1840, Doctor Livingstone sailed for the Society's distant mission station at Kuruman in South Africa.

Learning from the Africans

After a three-month voyage from Britain, Livingstone landed at Cape Town, South Africa, in March 1841. It took him another two months to complete the overland journey north to Kuruman, where he arrived at the end of July.

Livingstone was bitterly disappointed with Kuruman. He had heard the station's founder, Robert Moffat, speak of "the smoke of a thousand villages, where no missionary had ever been", and he expected to find Kuruman busy with African converts to Christianity since Moffat had been working there for 20 years. Instead he found that Kuruman was little more than a small village with fewer than 40 African converts. And there were no villages nearby.

With Moffat away in England, little was being done by the mission leaders at Kuruman. Livingstone found them jealous and quarrelsome, reluctant to push

deeper into Africa and unwilling to use African teachers to spread the Gospel more quickly. Naturally the mission leaders disliked the young newcomer's impatience with problems which they felt he could not yet fully understand.

Livingstone spent his early months at Kuruman learning the local **Sichuana** language from the Africans and testing his new skills as a doctor on native illnesses and injuries. But he decided that he could never stay at Kuruman, as the directors of the London Missionary Society had intended he should. To his sisters in Scotland Livingstone wrote "I would never build on another man's foundation. I shall preach the gospel beyond every other man's line of things."

▽ As Livingstone sets about learning the local Sichuana language from Africans at Kuruman, other mission leaders criticise his impatience with their missionary work – the result of Livingstone's inexperience.

A narrow escape

Between September and December 1841, Livingstone made the first of three journeys north-east from Kuruman. By June 1843 he had travelled some 805 kilometres deeper into the interior of Africa. The aim was to set up a new frontier **mission**, for which a site was finally chosen at Mabotsa.

With Roger Edwards, head of the Kuruman mission in Moffat's absence, Livingstone set off to establish the new

Mabotsa mission in August 1843. After three months Livingstone returned to Kuruman to meet Moffat, who had arrived from Britain with his wife and two daughters, Ann and Mary. Spending Christmas 1843 with the Moffats at Kuruman, Livingstone decided to propose marriage to Mary Moffat on his next visit to Kuruman. He was already feeling the loneliness of frontier missionary life.

Livingstone returned to Mabotsa and was working on the new mission when, on 16 February 1844, he had one of the narrowest escapes of his life. A lion attacked some of the villagers' sheep, and Livingstone went out to kill it. But his shots only wounded the lion, which attacked Livingstone before he had time to reload.

The lion knocked him down, grabbed him by the upper left arm and shook him "as a terrier dog does a rat". He was saved only by the bravery of Mebalwe, an African convert from Kuruman whom Livingstone had brought with him to Mabotsa to be a native teacher. Mebalwe and another African distracted the lion, which attacked them in turn and badly injured them before dropping dead, killed by the shots which Livingstone had fired.

With his arm splintered and gashed by the lion's teeth, Livingstone had no choice but to be his own doctor and set the bone himself. The wound caused him great suffering before it finally began to heal. On returning to Kuruman to rest and recover, Livingstone became engaged to Mary Moffat in May 1844.

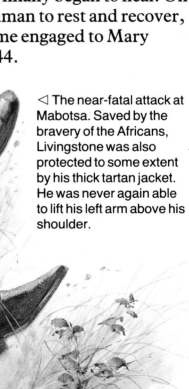

◁ The near-fatal attack at Mabotsa. Saved by the bravery of the Africans, Livingstone was also protected to some extent by his thick tartan jacket. He was never again able to lift his left arm above his shoulder.

▷ The Livingstone family visited England in 1857. Left to right: Oswell (born 1851); Thomas (born 1849); Agnes (born 1847), and Robert (born 1846). The fifth child, Anna Mary, was born in 1858. One child died in 1850.

▽ On his second crossing of the Kalahari, in 1850, Livingstone took his wife Mary (expecting her fourth child) and Robert (4), Agnes (3), and Thomas (1). Here he shows his family the Zouga River, flowing from Lake Ngami.

Across the Kalahari

After their wedding at Kuruman on 9 January 1845, the Livingstones spent the next three years moving on from one mission post to another. Livingstone was still hoping to set up a second, more successful Kuruman. But this was to remain a dream.

Mary Livingstone never knew a peaceful home in Africa for long. Livingstone expected his wife to share his travels and to run an African infant school at each new mission. There were frequent moves of home, and Mary also had to cope with having five children in six years.

David and Mary's journeys began after

he had many quarrels with Roger Edwards and decided that he would have to move on from Mabotsa. His first choice, in 1846, was Chonwane, 65 kilometres north of Mabotsa. Here the Livingstones stayed only 18 months before all the local water springs ran dry. The local chief, Sechele, led his people to new land at Kolobeng, 65 kilometres to the north-west, and the Livingstones travelled with them.

At Kolobeng Livingstone made his only conversion as a missionary when he baptised Chief Sechele in October 1848. Livingstone was bitterly disappointed when Sechele's conversion did not last six months. The chief refused to break tribal custom and give up his wives. But Kolobeng was a turning-point in Livingstone's life. It was from there that he made two journeys northwards across the Kalahari Desert, in 1849 and 1850. The experience changed him from a struggling missionary into an explorer.

Livingstone's goal was the mysterious Lake Ngami, said by Africans to lie north of the Kalahari. On his first journey (June–October 1849) a companion was the rich traveller William Cotton Oswell, who paid for the expedition. After crossing the Kalahari the men followed the Zouga River to Lake Ngami, learning of many other rivers to the north.

On the second journey (April–July 1850) Livingstone took Mary and their three young children. It was an astonishing risk to take considering Mary was expecting another baby. They reached Lake Ngami, but the baby girl who was born back at Kolobeng died when six weeks old.

▽ On 4 August 1851, Livingstone gazes across the upper Zambezi River, measuring 460 metres from bank to bank. "We thanked God", he wrote, "for permitting us to see this glorious river." He now decided to give his life to discovering the other "river highways" leading to the heart of central Africa.

14

The mighty Zambezi

The tragic death of baby Elizabeth did not stop Livingstone from taking his family on yet another journey across the Kalahari (April–September 1851). Again with Oswell's company, the party headed northwards across hundreds of kilometres of waterless land, guided by Africans. They were heading for the "land full of rivers" which Livingstone had been told lay north of the Zouga River.

Their sufferings were intense, but on 19 June they thankfully reached the banks of the Chobe River in the lands of the friendly Makololo people.

Livingstone and Oswell were warmly welcomed by Chief Sebetwane of the **Makololo**, but were badly shaken when he died only three weeks after their first meeting. It was a relief to find that the Makololo did not blame the strangers for the death of their chief.

Leaving Mary and the children in camp on the Chobe River, Livingstone and Oswell rode north, searching for a great river of which Sebetwane had told them. To cover the widest possible area they followed a zigzag course. On 4 August 1851 they were astounded to reach the upper Zambezi River, which Livingstone named "Shesheke" after the nearest village of the Makololo.

Livingstone's arrival on the Zambezi proved to the world that central Africa was not a barren desert, but a green and fertile land watered by many rivers. He hoped that these rivers would serve as highways along which traders and missionaries could sail, bringing wealth as well as Christianity to central Africa, thus freeing the Africans from slavery forever.

Inspired by these goals, Livingstone decided that he must spend the rest of his life putting these river highways on the map. He knew that his family could not come with him. Mary and the children sailed for England from Cape Town in April 1852. Five years were to pass before they met again – but when they did, Livingstone had become the most famous explorer in Britain.

West to the Atlantic

Between November 1853 and May 1856, Livingstone completed one of the most amazing journeys ever made. This was the first crossing of Africa from coast to coast, nearly 6,500 kilometres of mostly unexplored lands, passing through the countries that are known today as Angola, Zambia and Mozambique.

In all this time, apart from the handful of African porters who carried his food and equipment, Livingstone was alone. He kept going only by his courage and his faith that he was doing the work of God. Without his training as a doctor he would probably have died, for he often fell ill, usually with **malaria**. It was on this epic journey that Livingstone also proved his ability as a navigator. He made maps of his travels with an accuracy of detail and observation that still seems astonishing today.

After sadly bidding farewell to his family at Cape Town, Livingstone returned to the lands of the Makololo. His first aim was to follow the upper Zambezi as far west as he could, then head for Luanda in Portuguese Angola, on the Atlantic coast. This journey would, he hoped, discover a river route into the heart of Africa. This route could be used by the ships of traders and missionaries.

When they left the upper Zambezi, Livingstone and his little band pressed on to the west through forest and swamp. Sick with malaria, he reached Lake Dilolo on 20 February 1854, 1,525 metres above sea level. From here on, he noted, all the rivers flowed north and west – towards the Atlantic.

Ill and exhausted, Livingstone reached Luanda on 31 May 1854. He had originally thought that he would need 148 days to reach the coast. In fact he had taken 210 days.

◁ Wading up to their necks, the explorer's porters carry Livingstone through a swamp. Time and again it was their bravery and determination that made it possible for them all to continue the perilous journey.

▷ Livingstone takes a compass bearing to check his direction as he struggles through the gloomy undergrowth of a rain forest. The march to the Atlantic coast proved his great skills as a navigator.

17

"The smoke that thunders"

Livingstone spent nearly four months at Luanda, resting and writing letters and reports to the **London Missionary Society** and the **Royal Geographical Society**. Then, on 20 September 1854, he set off with his Makololo porters for the east. His aim was now to return to the upper Zambezi and follow the great river all the way to the Indian Ocean.

It took Livingstone nearly a year to cross Angola and return to the Makololo town of Linyanti. On the way he realised that Angola could never provide a route into central Africa for Europeans, because of the swarming tsetse flies which killed off the oxen used to pull wagons. He now hoped to prove that the Zambezi would provide a river highway into Africa from the Indian Ocean – but he already knew, from what the Makololo had told him, that there was at least one mighty waterfall on the Zambezi. The Makololo called it "Mosi-oa-Tunya" or "the smoke that thunders". Livingstone named this wonderful work of nature after the reigning queen of Great Britain, Queen Victoria, and it is still known today as the Victoria Falls.

Livingstone came to the Falls in wonder on 17 November 1855. Peering through the drifting spray and rainbows across the chasm into which the Zambezi thunders, he gave thanks to God. He wrote of the Falls that they "had never been seen before by European eyes, but scenes so lovely must have been gazed upon by angels in their flight".

After he left the Victoria Falls, it took Livingstone six more weary months to follow the Zambezi eastwards into Portuguese Mozambique, reaching the Indian Ocean coast at Quelimane on 20 May 1856. He believed that he had proved the Zambezi to be a water highway, but did not know that he had made a serious mistake. On the lower Zambezi Livingstone had taken a short cut overland across a loop of the river. By doing this he failed to discover the steep Kebrabasa Rapids, impossible to pass by boat.

Sailing from Quelimane in July 1856, Livingstone returned to Britain for the first time in 16 years, reaching home on 9 December.

◁ Livingstone reaches the Victoria Falls. He was greatly inspired by the magnificence of this sight.

△ Twice as high as America's Niagara Falls – the Victoria Falls as they are today.

The great lakes of Africa

When Livingstone returned to Britain in December 1856, he found that his exploits had made him a national hero. Britain's first man to cross Africa – it was almost like being the first man on the Moon. For the next year he toured the country, making speeches, receiving honours and writing a book (*Missionary Travels and Researches in South Africa*) which became a best-seller and provided him with money for further travels.

Livingstone argued that the time had come for a British expedition to open up the lower Zambezi to steamship traffic. At the same time a full-sized mission would convert the Makololo, his African friends and helpers on the upper Zambezi. Once the Makololo had been taught to grow cotton, sugar and indigo, the flow of British trade up the Zambezi would bring such profits that the slave trade would be finished for good. The British Government made Livingstone **Consul** for the Portuguese East African Coast. With high hopes he set out to lead an expedition up the Zambezi in March 1858.

▽ A strange new sight in the heart of Africa, in 1859. Livingstone's paddle-steamer *Ma-Robert*, named after his wife and eldest son, heads up the Shire River towards Lake Nyassa.

Livingstone's Zambezi expedition of 1858–1864 failed in all its major aims. Not good at working with a team of fellow Europeans, he quarrelled with all the expedition members – even his own brother, Charles. The Zambezi's Kebrabasa Rapids proved impassible to the lightest boats, and the mission to the Makololo also failed. Mrs Livingstone, who came out to join her husband, died of fever on the lower Zambezi on 27 April 1862. In the end the British Government, accepting that the Zambezi expedition had failed, recalled Livingstone in 1863.

Yet it was not a story of total failure. In 1859 Livingstone sailed his steam launch *Ma-Robert* ("Mother of Robert", the African name for Mrs Livingstone) northwards up the Shire River which flows into the lower Zambezi. The Shire led him to the southernmost of Africa's great lakes: Lakes Shirwa, Malombe and mighty Nyassa (known today as Lake Malawi).

From the moment of his recall from the Zambezi expedition in 1863, exploring the rivers flowing between the great lakes of Africa became Livingstone's main aim. These explorations lasted for the next ten years of his life.

Challenging the slave traders

Livingstone's Zambezi expedition, and the "Universities Mission to Central Africa" which came out to join it, soon ran into trouble with the authorities of Portuguese Mozambique. The Portuguese made money from the African slave trade, which Livingstone had vowed wholeheartedly to wipe out.

Though Livingstone did not believe in freeing slaves by violence, the new "Bishop of Central Africa", Charles Mackenzie, thought otherwise. He hated the fierce **Yao** tribesmen who rounded up their fellow-Africans for the slave trade, and he fought several battles to free their captives at gun-point. For this Livingstone was unfairly blamed by the British Government, after the Portuguese had protested to them.

By the time that Bishop Mackenzie died of malaria on 31 January 1862, the damage had been done. In the following year Bishop William Tozer, sent out to replace Mackenzie, brought the British Government's orders to Livingstone recalling the Zambezi expedition.

Livingstone now had to decide what to do with the steamboat *Lady Nyassa*, which he had hoped to carry in pieces to the great lake in order to cruise its waters and interrupt the slave trade. Knowing that the Portuguese would use the boat for carrying slaves if he sold it in Mozambique, Livingstone made an astonishing decision. Though *Lady Nyassa* could only carry enough coal for eight days' steaming, Livingstone decided to sail her all the way across the Indian Ocean, a voyage of over 3,200 kilometres, and sell her in Bombay.

It was a daring venture, for if the summer monsoon broke before Livingstone reached India, *Lady Nyassa* would surely sink in the wild weather. But after 45 days at sea, Livingstone sighted the Indian coast on 12 June 1864 and on the following day sailed into Bombay harbour – a great feat of navigation. He sailed for Europe on 24 June, and reached London on 23 July.

◁ Livingstone's beloved wife Mary, who came out to join him on the Zambezi and died of malaria on 27 April 1862. They had been married for 18 years.

▷ With guns at his back with which to fight only if necessary, Livingstone sternly opposes a party of slavers and orders the release of their captives from their wooden neck-yokes.

△ This drawing of slaves abandoned is a grim depiction of how slaves were mistreated and abused.

"Dr Livingstone, I presume"

After resting, writing a book about the Zambezi expedition and providing for his children, Livingstone sailed for Africa again in August 1865. It was a journey from which he was never to return. In the last eight years of Livingstone's life, growing concern for his safety and uncertainty about his whereabouts led to several expeditions being sent out to find him. The one which finally succeeded brought about one of the most famous meetings in history.

Since Livingstone's epic crossing of Africa, other British explorers had made important discoveries there. Richard Burton, John Speke, James Grant and Samuel Baker, searching for the sources of the Nile, had discovered the great lakes of Tanganyika, Victoria, Albert and Mweru, and the rivers which ran to and from them. However, there was still argument about where the true source of the Nile lay, and this Livingstone was now determined to find.

After collecting the Africans who had sailed with him to Bombay in *Lady Nyassa*, Livingstone landed at Zanzibar on 28 January 1866. His plan was to march inland from the coast to the Arab village of Ujiji, on the east coast of Lake Tanganyika. This would be his base for his journeys in search of the Nile's source. He travelled with a small party of African porters, depending on the British Consul and an Arab agent to send regular supplies from Zanzibar to Ujiji.

Marching inland on 6 April 1866, Livingstone reached Lake Nyassa on 8 August and headed slowly north towards Lake Tanganyika. He fell repeatedly ill,

△ As well as much-needed supplies, Stanley brought Livingstone news of the outside world. Here the two men enjoy reading the newspapers carried to Ujiji by Stanley's caravan.

◁ The famous meeting at Ujiji, with the tired and shabby figure of the great explorer in sharp contrast to Stanley's brand new equipment, sun helmet and shining boots.

and in January 1867 his medicine chest was stolen by two deserting porters. It was not until April 1867 that he reached Lake Tanganyika.

As the months became years with no firm news of his whereabouts, concern for Livingstone's safety continued to grow. In 1869 the owner of the American newspaper *New York Herald* sent out his most famous reporter, Henry Morton Stanley, with the simple order "Find Livingstone!"

It was on 10 November 1871 that Stanley reached Ujiji with a huge **caravan** loaded with supplies, with the American flag carried before him. As the tired and shabby figure of Livingstone came out to meet him, Stanley bowed, took off his hat, and spoke the famous words, "Dr Livingstone, I presume."

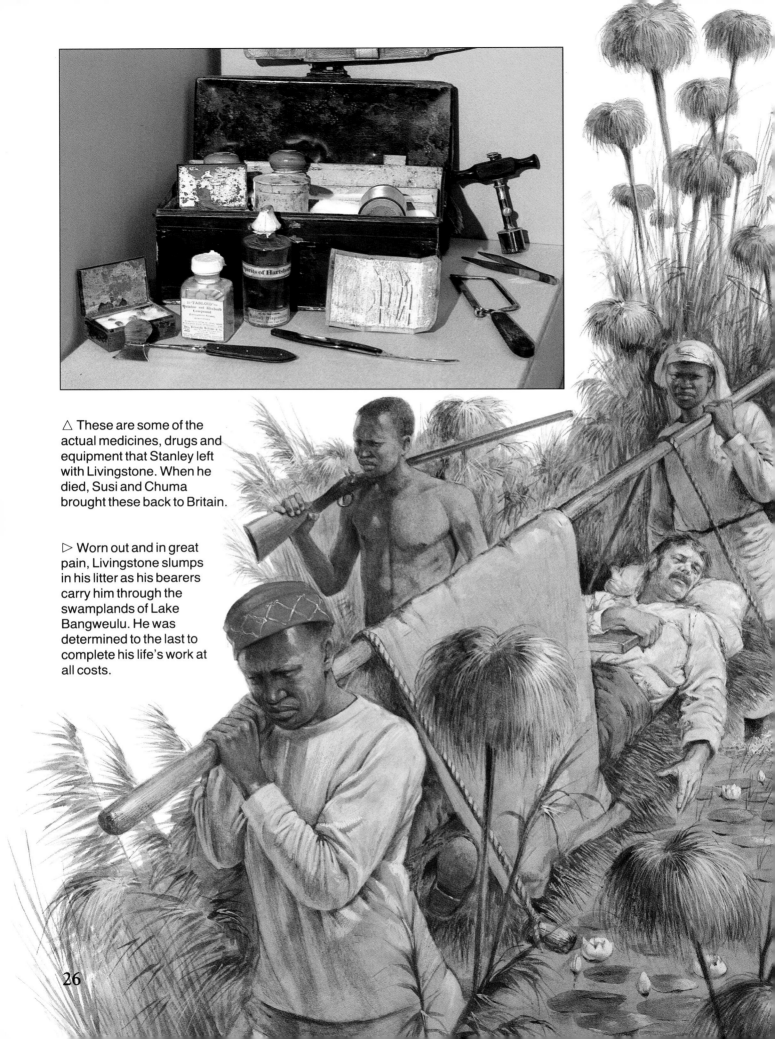

△ These are some of the actual medicines, drugs and equipment that Stanley left with Livingstone. When he died, Susi and Chuma brought these back to Britain.

▷ Worn out and in great pain, Livingstone slumps in his litter as his bearers carry him through the swamplands of Lake Bangweulu. He was determined to the last to complete his life's work at all costs.

The last march

Stanley had done more than just find Livingstone. He had saved his life. Livingstone had painfully returned to Ujiji in October 1871, to find that all the supplies that he had been expecting to find had been sold by an Arab to buy ivory. To Livingstone, Stanley's arrival was little less than a miracle. But he refused to go home with Stanley, insisting that his work was not yet finished.

The two men stayed together for three months, exploring the northern end of Lake Tanganyika. Then, on 14 March

1872, they parted. Taking Livingstone's journals and reports back to London, Stanley left Livingstone with enough medicines and supplies for four years. Stanley promised to send up a team of reliable porters from the coast, and when these finally arrived Livingstone set off on what proved to be his last march. It was 25 August 1872.

Livingstone was heading for his last great discovery: Lake Bangweulu, which he had found in July 1868. He had come to believe that the source of the Nile was a western branch of the Lualaba River, and that his goal therefore lay west of Lake Bangweulu. But in 1868 he had failed to make an accurate map of the huge marshes lying south of Lake Bangweulu. These errors were to cost him his life.

By the end of December 1872, enduring heavy rains, Livingstone's party was floundering through the Bangweulu swamps. Livingstone fell ill again, suffering from **dysentery**. His faithful African companions, Susi and Chuma, proved to be towers of strength, carrying the tired and suffering explorer across flooding rivers and through deep swamps in appalling weather.

"Rain, rain, as if it never tired", he wrote at the end of January 1873. But he refused to abandon the march. Five days after his sixtieth birthday he wrote in his diary, "Nothing earthly will make me give up my work in despair." By the end of April, suffering great pain, he could no longer mount his donkey. His loyal band carried him in a **litter** as they approached Chief Chitambo's village on the Lualaba River.

The "Great White Doctor" dies

On 29 April 1873, Livingstone's party reached Chitambo's village on the Lulimala. Livingstone was now suffering so much that further progress was impossible; he must rest.

On the night of 30 April, he recovered just enough to ask Susi for a cup of boiled water and a dose of **calomel**. His last words to Susi were a faint "All right, you can go now." Susi left Livingstone with a candle burning beside his bed.

Just before 4 o'clock in the morning, Susi was called in panic to Livingstone's bedside. He found that sometime in the night Livingstone had found the strength to climb out of bed. They found him slumped on his knees beside the bed, with his head between his hands. The "Great White Doctor" had ended his life in prayer.

Susi and Chuma prepared Livingstone's body for a burial that was assigned only to their African chiefs. His heart was removed and his body embalmed for the funeral in England. They set off on an epic march of 2,400 kilometres to Zanzibar. Carrying Livingstone's body, his papers and equipment, they finally arrived at Bagamoyo on the coast in February 1874.

It was fitting that Susi and Chuma travelled to England after the death of Livingstone. Unfortunately they arrived too late to attend his funeral in Westminster Abbey on 18 April 1874. His

△ The faithful Africans Susi and Chuma, who were photographed at Newstead Abbey, near Nottingham in 1874. With them are Livingstone's rifle, sword and cap and his Bible, maps, journals and notebooks.

courage and endurance had made him a
legend in his lifetime and had captured the
imagination of the world. "If ever a man
carried out the Scriptural injunction to
take no thought for the morrow," wrote
his old friend William Oswell, "that was
David Livingstone."

◁ Livingstone's red shirt was given to Stanley. Over the
years it has passed through Stanley's family; it is now
with the David Livingstone Centre.

▽ A great life has ended. The horrified Susi approaches
Livingstone's bedside to find that he has been dead for
several hours.

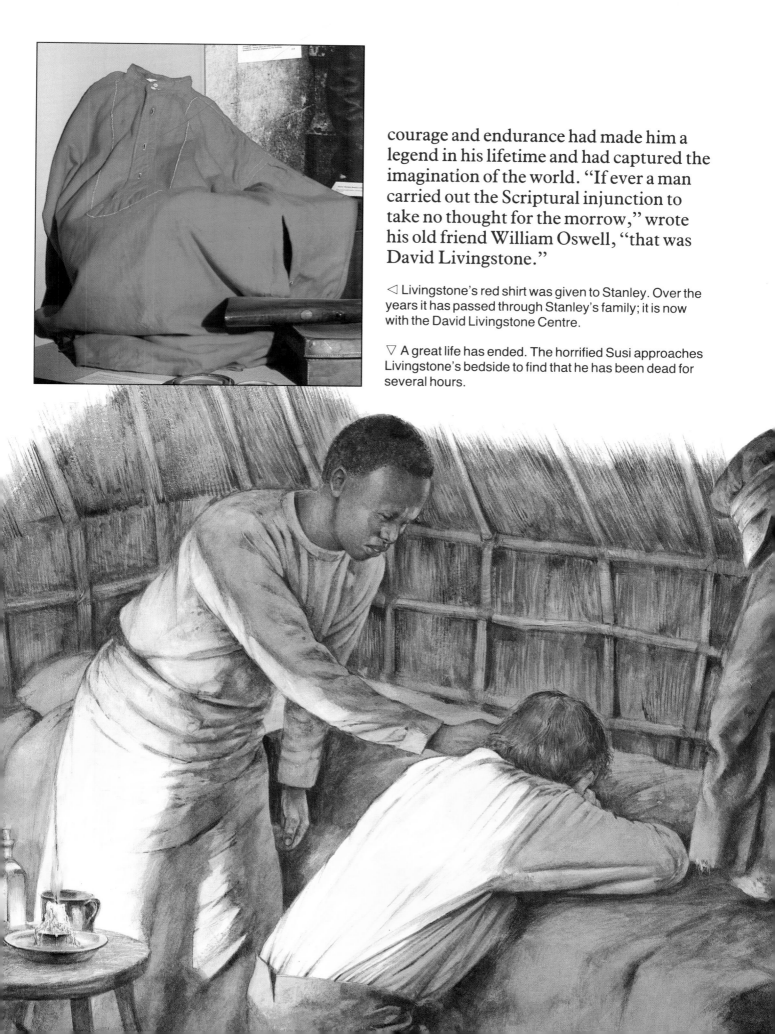

Glossary

Boers (Dutch for "farmers".) Familiar name for the Afrikaners, South African colonists of Dutch descent. They resented British rule and the work of British missionaries, believing that the black man was naturally inferior to the white.

Calomel Drug used to cure bowel disorders, with which Livingstone dosed himself during his last illness.

Caravan Large company of travellers, baggage animals, or human porters, formed for the safety of people and their goods while travelling through dangerous or unknown country.

Consul Official appointed to look after a country's citizens and interests in foreign lands. Livingstone was appointed British "Consul in the District of Quelimane on the Eastern Coast of Africa" before his return to the Zambezi in 1858.

Dysentery Exhausting and painful bowel disease which can kill by causing the body to lose too much fluid; one of the many diseases from which Livingstone suffered in Africa.

Litter Bed or hammock slung from a carrying-pole. Livingstone was carried in one when too ill to walk or ride on his

▷ Livingstone's travels and journeys of exploration in Central Africa lasted more than 30 years, and no man did more to open up the heart of the continent. This map of Livingstone's wanderings shows his last journey homewards: the devoted march to the coast at Zanzibar made by Susi and Chuma, carrying Livingstone's body home to his people.

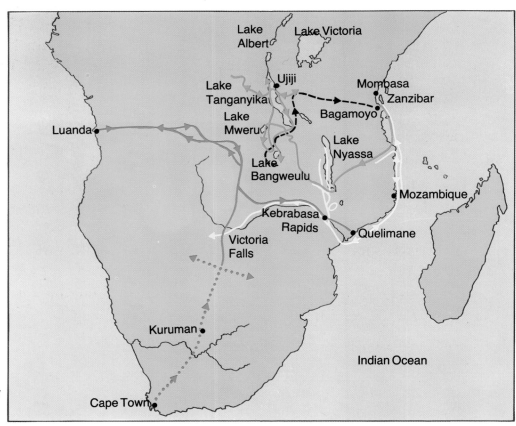

```
· · · · · ▶  1841–53
————▶  1853–56
————▶  1858–64
————▶  1866–73
– – – ▶  Susi, Chuma and
          Livingstone's body
```

last journey.

London Missionary Society Founded in 1795 to preach the Gospel in the world's wild places. The Society accepted Livingstone as a trainee missionary in 1838.

Makololo African tribe of the middle Zambezi, which provided Livingstone with a loyal team of porters for his famous crossing of central Africa in 1853–56.

Malaria Persistent, violent fever caused by the bite of mosquitoes; checked by regular doses of the drug quinine.

Mission Distant base for the preaching of Christianity. It usually consisted of the missionary's house and garden, with a small school. Mission stations were natural centres for exploration and trade.

Royal Geographical Society Leading British body for the encouragement of exploration, which supported the expeditions of Livingstone and others.

Sichuana The first of many native languages learned by Livingstone in Africa, spoken in the Kuruman region of northern Cape Colony and modern Botswana.

Yao A fierce African tribe of the Shire Plateau between Lake Nyassa and the lower Zambezi, active in the slave trade.

19 March 1813 David Livingstone born at Blantyre, Scotland.
8 December 1840 Livingstone sails for South Africa.
9 January 1845 Livingstone's wedding to Mary Moffat.
1849–51 Livingstone's crossings of the Kalahari Desert.
4 August 1851 Livingstone reaches the upper Zambezi River.
1853–56 Livingstone's crossing of Africa from Angola to Mozambique.
17 November 1855 Livingstone discovers the Victoria Falls.
1856–58 Livingstone hailed as a national hero in Britain.
1858–63 Failure of Livingstone's Zambezi expedition.
16 September 1859 Livingstone discovers Lake Nyassa.
27 April 1862 Death of Mary Livingstone.
2 July 1863 Recall of Zambezi expedition.
April–June 1864 Livingstone sails *Lady Nyassa* from Africa to India.
14 August 1865 Livingstone sails from England on his last expedition.
18 July 1868 Livingstone discovers Lake Bangweulu.
10 November 1871 H. M. Stanley finds Livingstone at Ujiji.
1 May 1873 Death of Livingstone.

Index

America 4, 19, 25
Angola 4, 16, 19, 31
Atlantic Ocean 16

Bagamoyo 28
Baker, Samuel 24
Blantyre 6, 31
Boers 4, 5, 30
Bombay 22, 24
Botswana 31
Britain 8, 19, 26, 31
Burton, Richard 24

calomel 28, 30
Cape Colony 4, 31
Cape Town 8, 15
caravan 25, 30
Chitambo, Chief 27, 28
Chobe River 15
Chonwane 13
Christianity 6, 8, 15, 31
Chuma 26, 27, 28, 30
Congo River 4
consul 20, 24, 30

Dark Continent 4
David Livingstone Centre 29
Diaz, Bartholomew 4
dysentery 27, 30

Edwards, Roger 10, 13
Egypt 4
England 8, 12, 15, 28, 31

Grant, James 24
Great Lakes 21, 24

India 22, 31
Indian Ocean 19, 22

Kalahari Desert 12, 13, 15, 31
Kebrabasa Rapids 19, 21
Kolobeng 13

Kuruman 6, 8, 9, 10, 11, 13, 31

Lake Bangweulu 26, 27, 31
Lake Dilolo 16
Lake Ngami 12, 13
Lake Nyassa 20, 21, 24, 31
Lake Tanganyika 24, 25, 27
Linyanti 19
litter 26, 27, 30
Livingstone, Charles 21
Livingstone, Mary 11, 13, 21, 31
Livingstone, Neil 6
London Missionary Society 6, 9, 19, 31
Lualaba River 27
Luanda 16, 19
Lulimala River 28

Mabotsa 10, 11, 13
Mackenzie, Bishop Charles 22
Makololo people 15, 16, 19, 20, 21, 31
malaria 16, 22, 31
Mebalwe 11
mission 10, 11, 13, 20, 21, 22, 31
Moffat, Ann 11
Moffat, Mary see Livingstone, Mary
Moffat, Robert 8, 10, 11
Mombasa 4
Mozambique 4, 16, 19, 22, 31

navigation 16, 22
Niagara Falls 19
Niger River 4
Nile River 4, 24, 27

Oswell, William Cotton 13, 15, 29

Quelimane 19, 30

Royal Geographical Society 19, 31

Scotland 6, 9, 31
Sebetwane, Chief 15
Sechele, Chief 13
Shesheke 15
Shire River 20, 21
Sichuana 9, 31
slave trade 4, 5, 15, 20, 22, 23
Sofala 4
South Africa 6, 8, 30, 31
Speke, John 24
Stanley, Henry Morton 25, 26, 27, 29, 31
Susi 26, 27, 28, 29, 30

Tozer, Bishop William 22
tsetse flies 19

Ujiji 24, 27, 31

Victoria Falls 19, 31
Victoria, Queen 19

West Indies 4
Westminster Abbey 28

Yao tribe 22, 31

Zambesi River 4, 14, 15, 16, 19, 20, 21, 30, 31
Zambesi Expedition 20, 21, 22, 24, 31
Zambia 16
Zanzibar 24, 28, 30
Zouga River 12, 13, 15

PRINTED IN BELGIUM BY

proost
INTERNATIONAL BOOK PRODUCTION